How Do Animals Use...
Their Eyes?

Lynn Stone

Rourke
Publishing LLC
Vero Beach, Florida 32964

www.rourkepublishing.com

PHOTO CREDITS: All Photos © Lynn Stone except pg. 15 © Mphoto.com

Editor: Robert Stengard-Olliges

Cover design by: Nicola Stratford bdpublishing.com

Library of Congress Cataloging-in-Publication Data

Stone, Lynn M.
  How do animals use their eyes? / Lynn Stone.
     p. cm. -- (How do animals use--?)
  ISBN 978-1-60044-504-0
  1. Eye--Juvenile literature. I. Title.
  QL949.S745 2008
  591.4'4--dc22
                                2007015160

Printed in the USA

CG/CG

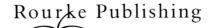

Rourke Publishing

www.rourkepublishing.com – rourke@rourkepublishing.com
Post Office Box 3328, Vero Beach, FL 32964

Animals use their eyes to see.

Wolf's eyes can see danger.

Eagle's eyes help it see fish.

Mountain lion's eyes can see its prey.

Bighorn sheep's eyes help it find grass to eat.

Owl's eyes can see at night.

13

Fish eyes can see underwater.

Butterflies eyes help it find flowers.

Duck's eyes help it see to swim.

Animals use their eyes to see many things.

21

Glossary

bighorn sheep (big horn sheep) – large mountain sheep with horns

butterfly (BUHT uhr flie) – an insect with two pairs of wings

duck (duhk) – a bird that swims and lives in water

eagle (EE guhl) – a big bird with long wings

fish (fish) – an animal that lives in water

mountain lion (MOUN tuhn LIE uhn) – a cougar that lives in the mountains

Index

Further Reading

Labella, Susan. *Owls and Other Animals with Amazing Eyes*. Children's Press, 2005.

Perkins, Wendy. *Let's Look at Animal Eyes*. Pebble Plus, 2007.

Websites

www.kidsites.com/sites-edu/animals.htm
animal.discovery.com

About the Author

Lynn M. Stone is the author of more than 400 children's books. He is a talented natural history photographer as well. Lynn, a former teacher, travels worldwide to photograph wildlife in its natural habitat.